BREAKING FREE

FROM

DEPRESSION

To Albert
With love
from Mom
2003

Psalms 94:19
God bless you always.

Charisma
HOUSE

LINDA MINTLE, PH.D.

BREAKING FREE FROM DEPRESSION by Linda S. Mintle, Ph.D.
Published by Charisma House
A part of Strang Communications Company
600 Rinehart Road
Lake Mary, Florida 32746
www.charismahouse.com

Cover design by Debbie Lewis
Interior design by David Bilby

Library of Congress Catalog Card Number:
2002108798

International Standard Book Number:
0-88419-893-6

This book is not intended to provide therapy, counseling, clinical advice or treatment or to take the place of clinical advice and treatment from your personal physician or professional mental health provider. Readers are advised to consult their own qualified healthcare physicians regarding mental health and medical issues. Neither the publisher nor the author takes any responsibility for any possible consequences from any treatment, action or application of information in this book to any reader. Names, places and identifying details with regard to stories in this book have been changed to protect the privacy of individuals who may have had similar experiences. The people referenced consist of composites of a number of people with similar issues, and the names and circumstances have been changed to protect their confidentiality. Any similarity between the names and stories of individuals described in this book to individuals known to readers is purely coincidental.

03 04 05 06 — 8 7 6 5 4 3 2
Printed in the United States of America

Remember that there is nothing stable in human affairs; therefore avoid undue elation in prosperity or undue depression in adversity.

—SOCRATES

Contents

"IT'S NO USE; MY LIFE IS O V E R."

"I really don't CARE anymore."

"SOMETIMES I WISH I COULD GO TO SLEEP AND
NEVER WAKE UP."

"All I do is cry."

*"It doesn't matter. Nothing will ever
change."*

**"I've had thoughts about killing
myself."**

"Nothing seems to be enjoyable anymore."

"It's like there is a cloud over my head."

"Why am I even HERE?"

"I CAN'T CONCENTRATE ANY-
MORE."

"Nobody cares!"

INTRODUCTION

When is sadness only sadness? And when does sadness become depression? How do you tell the difference? After all, everyone has the "blues" now and then.

Sadness is a normal reaction to any experienced loss, and it goes away with time. Your emotional makeup is such that you should feel sad when something goes wrong, someone gets hurt, a loved one dies, you break up with your girlfriend, your friend moves away or other issues involving loss occur.

But if you find yourself stuck in that sad feeling and unable to move on with life, you might be depressed. Depression affects the body, mood, thoughts and soul. It is more than normal sadness or feeling down. It's a persistent sadness that permeates most aspects of your life—sleeping, eating, working, communing with God, socializing and enjoying life. Depression is serious and debilitating, not something you just snap out of overnight. And it is not just "all in your head."

So if you think you suffer from depression, read on. It's time to start fully participating in life again and to replace that hopelessness with joy. Depressive feelings can be overcome. In this book, you will:

- Understand what depression is
- Learn about the different types of depression
- Examine biblical guidelines for dealing with depression
- Learn breaking free strategies to combat depression
- Practice and live a transformed life

Remember, depression doesn't have to disable you or hang over your head like a dark cloud. But you must take action. Doing nothing can be devastating. In the most serious cases, depression left unchecked can lead to suicide. So get help, and begin to walk in freedom today.

CAN YOU RELATE?

Jill

Jill can't get out of bed in the morning.

She's losing weight, has no appetite and can't concentrate at her job. About six weeks ago, she stopped working out at her sport club and lost interest in her photography club. Everything seems to irritate her. The other day her boss gave back an assignment, and she burst into tears.

Depression affects the body, mood, thoughts and soul.

"I can't seem to get control of my emotions," she says. "Lately I've thought of driving my car over a cliff."

Tim

Tim's father died unexpectedly. One month before at his father's sixty-eight birthday party, Tim joked that his dad would probably outlive him. The deadly heart attack surprised everyone in the family. The shock hit Tim hard. At first, he couldn't believe it. Then the grief came. Tim felt empty and very alone. Months went on, and Tim couldn't shake his sadness. He isolated and withdrew from friends and family. People began to worry. The once vibrant Tim looked thin and pale.

Rachel

Rachel was moody and depressed. She was competent at her job as an accountant, but she was losing interest in it. She felt hopeless about her future and annoyed with people. The more she complained, the worse she felt. But she could see no reason to be positive in her life. "Look at my life. Would you be happy? People only care about themselves. There is no one who loves me—either they die or take off. I must be undesirable, uninteresting and unable to attract healthy men. No one bothers with me. Life is a series of disappointments, and I'm tired of it."

Depression is a response to life's constant losses and challenges. We may face big losses, like a father diagnosed with cancer, the death of a spouse, a child in chronic pain, a catastrophic tornado, a deadbeat dad not paying child support or a love turned sour. Or we can sweat the small but significant stuff, such as a husband who rarely says "I love you," a critical boss, a mother-in-law who meddles, a heartless friend or the woman who gets in the express grocery line with thirty items in her cart! The list could go on forever.

Put simply, depression can result from not dealing well with people, circumstances and expectations. In many cases, we bring on depression by the way we respond. Other times depression is the cause of poor responding. So let's begin by understanding what depression is and how we can break free from this condition.

> *Depression is a response to life's constant losses and challenges.*

B R E A K I N G  F R E E

P R A Y E R   F O R   Y O U

Lord, I don't want to live my life feeling depressed all the time. I want to break free from depression. I am willing to do whatever it takes. I trust You to heal me. You are able to deliver me.

CHAPTER 1

UNDERSTANDING DEPRESSION

Into each life some rain must fall; some days be dark and dreary.

—HENRY WADSWORTH
LONGFELLOW

Depression is a mood disorder that affects more than eighteen million Americans.[1] Serious depression debilitates the individual and can tear apart families. However, depression is treatable. Unfortunately, most people who have depression don't get help. Life becomes a drudgery and not worth waking up for in the morning. But there is hope. And the first step is to ask for help and believe for healing.

As we move through life, we often get stuck in three primary areas—our relationships, our circumstances and/or our

1

expectations and dreams. As we face disappointments, unforeseen events and people who don't behave in ways that are loving, depression can set in. We may not be aware that daily struggles can trip us up, because we expect only the big things like death, divorce and disease to bring on depressed feelings.

> *A depressed mood negatively affects your perception of the world, which then feeds your negative thinking.*

But we face relationship difficulties, out-of-control circumstances and failed expectations almost daily. Some examples include dealing with a husband who puts work over family time, a company that passes you over for a promotion, not making the kind of income you thought you would at this stage in life, comparing yourself to others or failing an exam. These losses can trigger negative thinking, which brings on a depressed mood. A depressed mood negatively affects your perception of the world, which then feeds your negative thinking. This cycle of thinking negatively, feeling depressed and viewing the world from a negative lens goes round and round and keeps depression alive.

 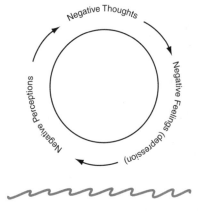
The Depression Cycle

Negative thinking is behind most depression. It is usually based on lies we believe, such as, "The situation is hopeless." "I'll never be able to change." "I'm unloved." It almost always involves a negative view of the self, the world and/or the future. Once we break the lies associated with this negativity, we can be free.

Who Gets Depressed?

"Christians should never get depressed!" Believe it or not, people say this! How wrong it is to make this kind of judgment, especially since it is hurtful and born out of ignorance. As you will learn, there are many causes of depression—sometimes directly related to spiritual issues, other times not.

For example, people can become depressed when they are disobedient and living in rebellion to God's Word. I once saw a Christian woman in therapy for several months whose depression was not lifting no matter what we tried. As I probed for root causes, I discovered she was secretly having sexual relations with a man in her singles group at church. She was too embarrassed to tell me, knowing the behavior was wrong. Once she repented and agreed to stop this behavior, the depression left. In her case, sin and the guilt associated with it were the roots of her depression. Until she stopped sinning, nothing changed.

But rebellion is not always the cause of depression. More often, negative thinking is the culprit. It develops out of life experiences. People who suffer sexual abuse, grow up in the homes of alcoholics, live through messy divorces, lose a

When depression hits, your relationship with God is usually depressed as well.

loved one to death, cope with chronic illness or experience financial problems often experience trauma, abuse, abandonment or neglect. These experiences make us vulnerable to the lies of the enemy. He tries to discourage and convince us that life is hopeless. Our minds are fertile ground for attack when our defenses are down. Because we hurt, we give him entry.

When depression hits, your relationship with God is usually depressed as well. God seems far away or uninterested. You believe He is unable or doesn't want to help you. This leads to despair. Part of the work is to restore your belief that God is working for you despite the troubles around you. He still cares and wants you whole. In fact, He is your healer.

As we confront loss, life transitions, medical conditions and other possible causes of depression, God is with us. He cares about our spiritual, emotional and physical health.

Depression in the elderly

Contrary to popular belief, it is not normal to be old and depressed. We tend to dismiss depression in the elderly, thinking they are just upset about aging. Actually, most elderly people feel fairly satisfied with their lives. However, depression can set in, given health changes and other issues related to aging. Those who take medications for physical problems can experience depression as a side effect. Certain medical conditions may even cause depression. And of course, depression in the elderly can be caused by the same problems that younger people face—the death of a spouse or other losses, medical conditions, unresolved anger, negative thinking and other factors.

Depression in children

Children can be depressed, although they don't always look the same as an adult with depression. For example, children may pretend to be sick, refuse to go to school, cling to a parent or worry that a parent may die. Older children may get in trouble at school or be agitated and restless. Look for signs of gloom, loss of interest in activities, low self-esteem, irritability, school underachievement, social withdrawal, appetite changes, sleep difficulties, concentration and excessive tiredness.

The question most parents ask is, "Is my child just going through a temporary mood phase, or is he depressed?" If you think your child may be depressed, arrange a complete physical examination in order to rule out any possible medical reasons for mood changes first. Then get a mental health evaluation to determine if your child or teen is depressed.

New mothers

News reports have made us more aware of *postpartum depression*. You may know someone like Kelly who, weeks after the delivery of her baby, sobs, "I'm not a good mother. I have thoughts of hurting my baby, and I feel like running away from home. I thought motherhood would be this wonderful experience. All I do is cry over little things. Yesterday I was mad because my husband made the bed the wrong way. What's wrong with me?"

What's wrong is that Kelly is experiencing a serious mood disorder that affects 10–20 percent of new moms.[2] It's sometimes called the "baby blues" and was previously known as *postpartum* ("after birth") *depression*. However, it is more severe than the blues and lasts for a longer time.

There are actually three types of postpartum conditions. The most common is *postpartum blues*. About 60–80 percent of new mothers feel down and "blue" within three days following birth. Mild symptoms of depression last a few days or a few weeks.[3]

Postpartum depression, like Kelly's, is more serious and often affects the new mother three to six months after birth. But it can begin as late as up to a year after delivery. Signs of depression are present.

Postpartum psychosis is the severest form and only affects about 0.1 percent of women who give birth.[4] Symptoms are severe and include confusion, suspicion, mania and seeing things that aren't there. Medical treatment is needed because of the potential harm to both the mother and baby.

When you consider the magnitude of change that women experience after childbirth, it is no wonder these mood disorders are so common. Hormone levels change, sleep is disrupted, new stress emerges and the entrée into motherhood begins. And if there were other stresses before the arrival of the baby, the entire experience can be overwhelming.

Symptoms of postpartum depression include sadness, chronic crying, lethargy, lack of motivation, anxiety, severe insomnia, loss of appetite, loss of sexual interest, mental confusion, inability to concentrate, forgetfulness, feelings of desperation, hopelessness, withdrawal, anxiety, chest-pounding panic attacks and, in severe cases, suicide and infanticide.

These disorders are not fully understood,

but are classified as *hormonally based psychological disorders* because they have a psychological, social, biochemical and hormonal component. They can recur in subsequent pregnancies.

MARRIAGE AND DEPRESSION

Although depression is typically thought of as an individual disorder (sometimes biologically based), depression can be triggered by marital distress. Whether they cause or maintain depression, distressed marriages are particularly difficult for women.

Women in unhappy marriages are more likely than men to be depressed. In part, this is because women highly value relationships and their roles as wives. When marital relationships are satisfying, women do better.

Women also tend to accommodate the needs of others to the exclusion of their own needs. As a result, they can feel isolated and frustrated and can lose their sense of self. This "loss of self" can lead to depression.

Life stress and marital arguments can also set off depression. Once depressed, the spouse often solicits negative reactions from the other spouse. Then a vicious cycle of stress, aggravated by depressed feelings and actions and negative exchanges between spouses, can create more hostility and detached feelings. The spouse that is not depressed tends to be more critical of the depressed spouse, leaving him or her feeling bad.

Other marital dynamics that set up depression are the lack of spousal support, the inability to confide in a spouse and an absence of emotional expression. In these cases, spouses should become more mutually supportive and more emotionally expressive. Spouses can learn to work together to solve problems, thus feeling less isolated. The result is improved marital relationships and mental health.

If you are a married, depressed person, include your spouse in your healing.

The bottom line is this: If you are a married, depressed person, include your spouse in your healing. The more involved he or she is, the more you can work on specific couple issues that may cause or maintain the depression of one spouse. Don't assume that the individual symptoms of one partner are unrelated to the other. You may not be right! In many cases, improving the couple relationship is the key to overcoming depression.

In general, however, being married helps, especially men. When you compare married people to divorced and singles, married people have less depression.

Types of Depression

The word *depression* is a general word used to describe a number of types of depression. The most common types are major depression, dysthymia, adjustment disorder, bipolar depression and seasonal affective disorder (SAD).[5]

Major depression

Major depression involves a number of symptoms. You may feel chronically sad, hopeless, worthless and helpless. You may lose interest in things that used to be pleasurable. You may also lack energy, have difficulty concentrating and remembering, develop sleep problems, experience appetite changes and feel restless, irritable and suicidal. This kind of depression can happen once in a person's life or be repeated. It is usually severe and persists for at least two weeks, causing interference in daily living activities. In some cases, the depression may include suicidal thoughts or behaviors and/or even psychotic symptoms in which the person is out of touch with reality and not thinking clearly.

Dysthymia

Dysthymia is a type of depression that can lead to major depression or just linger for years. It is a milder form of depression that stays with you most of the time. Dysthymia is a chronic low-grade depression that causes distress and creates problems in living life to the fullest. This depressed state hangs on for at least a two-year period. People with dysthymia experience appetite changes, low energy, sleep difficulties, low self-esteem and feelings of helplessness and hopelessness.

Adjustment disorder

Adjustment disorder is another type of

depression that occurs as a response to a single event or situation. Usually there is one identifiable stress or series of stresses that set the depression in motion. Symptoms usually develop within three months of the stress event(s) and resolve before six months' time, or when the stress is no longer present. For example, this type of depression can result from a breakup with a boyfriend, a marital problem, a financial crisis or a divorce.

Bipolar depression

Bipolar depression, formerly known as *manic-depression*, is not as common as the other types, but it is serious. It can worsen to a psychotic state if not treated. This type of depression involves mood changes that cycle. For example, a person feels that she is flying high (mania) and then feels extremely down (depression). These mood changes can be gradual or dramatic and fast. In the depressed cycle, you can experience all the symptoms of depression—the most serious being suicidal thoughts that can lead to a suicide attempt. In the manic cycle, you may be overactive, talkative, elated, unable to sleep and irritable. You may feel increased sexual desires, or you may exercise poor judgment and inappropriate social behavior. Grandiose thoughts may race through your mind. The mania can cause embarrassment and serious problems. I've had clients who, during a manic episode, have acted out sexually, spent money impulsively, called strangers in the middle of the night and driven for miles to unknown places.

Recently several genes have been identified that may be related to bipolar depression. There is no known cure for bipolar depression, but the symptoms can be managed, and people can live a full, productive life. And, of course, with God healing is always possible.

Seasonal affective disorder (SAD)

Seasonal affective disorder (SAD) is a type of depression related to changes in the seasons and decreasing amounts of natural sunlight as the days get shorter. Known as the "winter blues," depression is activated by decreasing daylight. It usually begins mid-October and ends around April.

SAD is a treatable depression that affects about 35 million Americans. The farther north you live, the greater your chance to be one of the 10 million people diagnosed, or one of 25 million that have some symptoms. People in the northern states get half as much sunshine as those in the South.[6]

Sometimes the causes of depression can be easily seen. At other times depression seems to spring out of nowhere.

Symptoms can include tiredness, irritability, inability to concentrate, weight gain, craving carbohydrates, isolation and difficulty getting out of bed in the morning. Women in their thirties are most susceptible to SAD, but the disorder affects men and children, too.[7]

CAUSES OF DEPRESSION

Sometimes the causes of depression can be easily seen. At other times depression seems to spring out of nowhere. There may be one or multiple causes for a type of depression. Stress, heredity and genetics all play a role.

Common Causes of Depression

Here are common causes of depression:

- Loss (relationships, circumstances and situations, expectations and dreams)

- Significant life transitions

- Chronic medical conditions

- Physical changes in the body—stroke, heart attack, cancer, hormonal disorders

- Personality traits such as perfectionism, pessimism and being overly dependent

- Stressful changes in life patterns

- Unresolved anger

- Unrepentant sin and disobedience

- Occult involvement

- Negative thinking patterns

- Multiple stressors or feeling over-whelmed by stress

- Side effects of medications (high blood pressure, steroids and others)

- Alcohol and drug intoxication and withdrawal

- Diet—specifically, low levels of folic acid and vitamin B_{12}[8]

- Degenerative neurological conditions such as Alzheimer's and Huntington's disease

- Viral infections such as hepatitis and mononucleosis

Some people are more prone to depression because of their biological and genetic makeup. Researchers are unclear as to whether depression causes or is the result of brain chemistry changes. But we do know that brain chemistry changes. That's why antidepressant medications improve mood.

We also know that if you have a family history of depression, you are more at risk.

Depression runs in families. However, depression occurs in people with no family history of the disorder as well.

B R E A K I N G  F   R   E   E

P R A Y E R   F O R   Y O U

Lord, help me to understand depression and not to give up hope to be healed. It is not Your intention for me to live under such heaviness and hopelessness. In You there is freedom and the promise of an abundant life. It is my desire to be free of depression and to live in Your love and acceptance.

CHAPTER 2

IDENTIFYING DEPRESSION AND SUICIDE RISK

This is my depressed stance. When you're depressed, it makes a lot of difference how you stand. The worst thing you can do is straighten up and hold your head high because then you'll start to feel better. If you're going to get any joy out of being depressed, you've got to stand like this.

—CHARLIE BROWN

There isn't a biological or physical test you can take to determine if you are depressed. However, there are clear signs and symptoms. In addition, depression can be measured through self-report tests or interview measures. Physicians and mental health professionals can evaluate you if you are unsure. It's also important to talk about any suicidal feelings or thoughts you may have.

BREAKING FREE

MENTAL HEALTH FACT

How Do I Know If I'm Depressed?

Listed below are some of the signs to look for to know if you are suffering from depression. Usually five or more of these signs are present for a period of two weeks or more:

- Feeling sad and anxious, in a depressed mood
- Loss of interest or pleasure in activities
- Weight changes with changes in appetite
- Sleep changes (more or less than usual)
- Agitation
- Fatigue and loss of energy
- Feeling worthless, with inappropriate guilt
- Problems concentrating; indecisiveness
- Suicidal thoughts and/or plans[1]

Risk factors include marital distress, history of physical or sexual abuse, economic deprivation, social skill problems and lack of self-management skills.[2]

TEEN SUICIDE

Suicide is obviously the most serious response to depression someone can have. While suicide happens among all ages and groups of people, it is a special concern for teens and young adults. Suicide is now the third leading cause of death among people ages thirteen to twenty-four. According to a recent survey of high school students, teens (60 percent) often think about killing themselves, and some (9 percent) say they have made an attempt at least once. In the past three decades, teen suicide has risen 300 percent.[3]

BREAKING FREE
MENTAL HEALTH FACT

Suicide Risk Factors

Frank A. Jones Jr., M.D., at the University of

Medicine and Dentistry of New Jersey Robert Wood Johnson Medical School, lists these risk factors for suicide:

- Male
- Gay, lesbian, bisexual
- Divorced, single, separated, widowed
- A teen or elderly
- Someone who lives alone or who is socially isolated
- White, Native American
- A physician, psychologist, psychiatrist, dentist, police officer, attorney
- Unemployed
- Experiencing major depression
- Experiencing chronic emotional or physical pain
- Terminally ill
- Have lost physical function including neurological disorders
- Have loss of body parts or physical integrity
- Have HIV and AIDS
- In need of dialysis and dependent on others for healthcare
- Have a history of prior attempts
- Have a family history of prior suicides

- Have a history of physical, sexual or drug abuse[4]

DEPRESSION CAN LEAD TO SUICIDE

Courtney was found in her bed. Her parents were horrified as they stared at the empty pill bottle on the floor. Her diary read, "I don't want to bother anyone anymore. There is nothing left for me to live for. Maybe death will bring me some peace."

Courtney believed a lie that has gripped the hearts of many teens. They are deceived into thinking that the only solution to ending their life struggles is death. They have no hope for a better day. The feeling of hopelessness is often brought on by some disconnect, wounding, trauma or event in their lives. They are teens at risk for suicide.

Suicide is now the third leading cause of death among people ages thirteen to twenty-four.

It's normal for teens to be moody and dramatic. One moment they are on top of the world, the next, in despair. When you think about the pressures of modern life (divorce, family alcoholism, domestic violence, sexual abuse, competition for good grades and college entrances, violence in the media, increased access to guns and pills and other stresses), it's not hard to understand how a depressed teen could contemplate suicide.

Depression is behind suicide. It is a profound state of unhappiness that affects a person's functioning. As noted, it can be spiritually, emotionally and biologically based. Signs of teen depression are sleeping more than usual, not sleeping well and feeling tired, appetite changes, restlessness, isolation from friends and family, concentration problems, losing interest in activities, hopeless and guilt feelings, sudden mood changes, changes in grades and health and a feeling that life isn't worth living. If these changes and a depressed mood last longer than two weeks, more serious depression could result.

Many teens feel lonely, helpless and rejected due to parent disinterest, broken households, family problems and limited family time. Suicidal teens will tell you,

"My family doesn't understand me. They ignore or deny my feelings."

Loss can trigger thoughts of suicide— including parents' marital discord, separation or divorce; a humiliating circumstance involving family or friends; being abused; having parents who are substance abusers; doing poorly on a test; being excluded or a breakup with a boyfriend or girlfriend.

The feeling of hopelessness is often brought on by some disconnect, wounding, trauma or event in teens' lives.

Others at risk are pregnant teens, runaways and substance abusers. Sometimes there is no obvious stress, but the teen still feels depressed.

BREAKING FREE

MENTAL HEALTH FACT

Teens at Risk

Here are some questions to ask in order to decide if a teen is at risk for suicide:

- *Is there a family history of suicide?* Teens often identify with those close to them and repeat their actions.

- *Does he talk about suicide?* If a teen talks about suicide, take it seriously.

- *Has there been a previous suicide attempt?*

- *Are there signs of depression?* Signs may include changes in appetite, changes in sleep habits, loss of concentration, irritability, restlessness, withdrawal and isolation, declining grades, undue guilt, loss of interest in normal activities, mood changes or a wish to die.

- *Does he abuse substances?* Alcohol abuse is linked to suicide.

- *Is he acting out violent feelings?*

- *Does he feel hopeless, rejected or alone?*

- *Is he giving away favored possessions?*

- *Has he been abused physically or sexually?*

- *Is there a cheerful upswing after a bout of depression,* which could be caused by a decision to die and escape the pain of living?

- *Has there been a recent loss* like a parent's divorce, separation, custody change, a move, a death, a breakup with boyfriend or girlfriend?

- *Does he suffer from severe loss of self-esteem?*

- *Is he withdrawing from those to whom he was close?*

- *Does he have major peer problems?*

- *Is there a downward dive in school performance?*

- *Is there a chemical imbalance or other mental illness?*

- *Is there a chronic physical illness?*

- *Is there a dramatic change in personality and/or appearance?*

- *Is she pregnant and not coping well?*

- *Is he a runaway?*

- *Does he write about death?*

- *Does he have many psychoso-matic complaints?*

- *Has he been humiliated in front of family and friends?*

- *Does he have substance-abusing parents?*

- *Is his family life filled with strife?*

- *Is he rebellious in a serious way?*

- *Is there a sudden recklessness?*

- *Does he feel unloved?*

If you see any of the signs listed above in any teen you know, professional help should be considered. You may have a depressed teen who is thinking about suicide. With help, suicide is preventable. Your teen needs healing. The decision to die is based on a lie from the pit of hell. The devil's purpose is to steal, kill and destroy.

Sometimes, as parents, we feel over-whelmed by the dangers our teens face. No matter how we try to protect them, they live in a world filled with messages counter to the Christian faith. But there is hope, and there is much you can do to help a depressed and suicidal teen. You are not powerless. God is mighty and can speak truth to any hopeless situation.

B R E A K I N G F R E E

M E N T A L H E A L T H F A C T

Preventing Teen Suicide

Here are some steps you can take to prevent your teen from becoming a statistic:

- *Talk with your teen about his suicidal feelings.* Talking about suicide does not cause someone to do it. Ask if they have a plan. If they do, they are more at risk.

- *Don't promise to keep suicidal feelings a secret.* Make it clear that people must be told so that help can be given.

- *Communicate that there is a way out of whatever she faces.* Suicidal teens are convinced that killing themselves is the only answer. Options need to be presented. The lie of hopelessness must be confronted.

- *Don't lecture. Listen.* Teens will talk if you listen. Make yourself available.

- *Reassure him that he is not a burden.* Assure them you want to hear what they are thinking and feeling and will take it seriously.

- *Remove any means for self-harm.* If there are guns, pills, knives or ropes available for harm, get rid of them.

- *Identify the lie that is telling her to self-destruct, and ask God to reveal the truth to her.*

- *Speak the Word of God into his life.*

- *Pray and intercede.* You and others should lift teens in prayer. If they don't have personal relationships with Jesus, introduce them.

- *Teach her the Word of God.* Scripture is a powerful weapon against any attack. Fill your teen so full of the Word that she recognizes the truth. The truth will set her free. Begin at an early age.

- *Tell your teen that he is loved unconditionally.* Communicate that there is nothing he can do to make you stop loving him.

- *Spend time with your teen.* The single best prevention against any teen risk behavior is a meaningful relationship with a parent. Be there. Know your teen. Be involved.

- *Be direct.* Problems aren't solved by death. Instead people are hurt. Discuss how those alive suffer.

- *Give hope.* God will never leave or forsake that teen. Ask God to reveal His truth whenever the lie of self-destruction appears.

- *Get professional help.* Suicidal teens suffer from depression. They may need intervention from people trained to work with depression and/or suicide issues.

There are many sources of help. Check your local mental health agencies, and ask for Christian therapists trained to treat teen depression and suicide. Involve your church youth leaders as prayer partners. If you don't know where to begin, contact your family physician, pastor or community services.

BREAKING  FREE
PRAYER FOR YOU

Lord, help me to identify the lies that lead to depression and suicidal thinking. Then speak Your truth to me. You are a God of life and joy, not of destruction and lies. Help me to recognize the real enemy of my soul, who wants to steal my joy and destroy me. Your plans for me are good. You created me and gave me life. I want to live. You unconditionally love me—any message counter to that is a lie.

CHAPTER 3

BIBLICAL TRUTH REGARDING DEPRESSION

...to proclaim the year of the LORD's favor and the day of vengeance of our God, to comfort all who mourn, and provide for those who grieve in Zion—to bestow on them a crown of beauty instead of ashes, the oil of gladness instead of mourning, and a garment of praise instead of a spirit of despair. They will be called oaks of righteousness, a planting of the LORD for the display of his splendor.

—ISAIAH 61:2-3

People in the Bible suffered depression and despair. One only has to read the Book of Psalms to understand the spiritual journey of so many. In this book, ordinary people struggle to experience what they believe about God. Their stories filled with trust and revealing moments of feeling abandoned resound with our own life experiences.

Just read through Book of Psalms, and you will find feelings of paranoia, doubt, hatred, betrayal, revenge and then joy, delight and praise—all mixed up and representing our struggle with God who is good, but who allows us to live and function in a fallen world.

David, who embodied so many emotions we all feel from time to time, steadfastly believed that he mattered to God. Not only did he

God does not want you depressed.

believe, but he also experienced the living God. As he cried out in despair, God touched him.

God does not want you depressed. He wants you experiencing His joy no matter the circumstances of your life. How is this possible when you feel depressed or cast down? Psalm 43 tells you to hope in God and praise Him, and He will help you.

In order to combat feelings of hopelessness associated with depression you must believe there is always hope in God. The enemy tells you there is no way out of your situation or no solution to your problem. He is a liar, because God says this isn't so. His promise is to make a way where there is no way and to be your help in the time of trouble. He is your refuge. Trust in Him.

> But he said to me, "My grace is sufficient for you, for my power is made perfect in weakness." Therefore I will boast all the more gladly about my weaknesses, so that Christ's power may rest on me. That is why, for Christ's sake, I delight in weaknesses, in insults, in hardships, in persecutions, in difficulties. For when I am weak, then I am strong.
>
> —2 CORINTHIANS 12:9-10

If you feel hopeless, read the promises of God *and verbalize them.* Change your thoughts from negative and hopeless to positive and hopeful because of Christ in you. You are His son or daughter. Like any good parent, He wants the best for you.

The voice of depression is hopeless, anxious and negative—all counter to the Word of God. When you listen to the voice of depression, you give the enemy a stronghold, an area of your life in which to defeat you. He lies and deceives. <u>You must replace negative thoughts with God's truth, act in loving ways and think on the promises of God.</u>

How do you do this? In order to change your thoughts, you must renew your mind. The first step is to identify the lie that is telling you that your situation or life is hopeless.

God's promise is to make a way where there is no way.

Once you identify that lie, ask God to speak His truth to you regarding the specific lie. According to the Bible, it is the truth that sets us free. John 14:6 tells us that Jesus is the way, *the truth* and the life. He is able to bring truth to all enemy deception.

The Scripture also says that <u>your help comes from the Lord. Stop putting your trust in those around you, and go directly to God in prayer.</u> Call on His name, and

He will answer. Work with a godly counselor, but recognize that God is the source of your help. You have to spend time in the Word and prayer in order to be with your heavenly Father. Don't just read and think about God. Experience Him. Then, allow the Word to renew your mind.

Think about the despair and hopelessness you feel. Let yourself feel it for a moment. As you feel this depression, try to identify the lie associated with this feeling. What comes into your head? What thought is automatic? It may be something like, *I'll never be happy. No one cares about me.* As you think that thought, ask Christ to tell you His truth. He is the light that can pierce the darkness that you feel. He will speak to you if you ask Him to do so. When He does, His truth will renew your thinking.

Praise is the antidote to feeling down and depressed.

Then praise Him. The Bible says, "His praise shall continually be in my mouth" (Ps. 34:1, NKJV). When we praise, we use a powerful weapon against the enemy. Our

God is worthy of praise, because He is greater than the enemy. He has already defeated Satan.

The Bible also tells us to put on "a garment of praise instead of a spirit of despair" (Isa. 61:3). This means that *we* have to praise willfully even when we don't feel like it. We clothe ourselves in the praises of God. When we do, the heaviness begins to lift. Praise is the antidote to feeling down and depressed. Don't wait until you *feel* like praising because you may not. Just do it.

Don't praise God for the depression; it isn't from Him. Praise Him because He knows the depths of your despair. He nailed your depression to the cross. Because of Calvary, you are already free.

BREAKING 🕊 FREE

MENTAL HEALTH FACT

Praise Steps

- Stand on His Word.
- Spend time with your Father.
- Believe He is your hope.

- Go to Him for help.
- <u>Ask Jesus to reveal the lies that enslave you and to set you free with His truth.</u>
- Praise Him because He's already done everything you need.

VALUE THINGS THAT ARE ETERNAL

We have all lost things that were valuable. When I was a child, I lost my favorite Disneyland ring. It was only a five-dollar fake pearl, but it was my cherished prize. To me, it was valuable. It was a special gift from a place I loved.

Guarding it carefully on the trip home from California to Michigan, I took extra precautions. As a child, I thought that washing the ring would somehow ruin it, so I took it off and placed it on a restroom sink in Montana. Unfortunately, I forgot to put it back on my finger again. One state later, I remembered where I left that ring. I thought I would never recover from the loss.

Loss is difficult to face whether you are seven or sixty-five. Things have a way of taking on meaning in our lives. When we lose them, we struggle. The problem with things is that having them—and keeping them—is not always in our control. We can lose things through disasters like accidents, floods, tornadoes or fire. We can lose things like money or houses by making bad decisions. Other things are lost through no fault of our own.

Things aren't as important as we make them out to be. We give them value far beyond what they deserve. Losing things becomes traumatic when we have trusted in *things* to make us happy or to give us security. In fact, we can get depressed over losing things.

God wants us to value things that are eternal, not to value the material goods of this world. He wants our dependency and will give us every good thing we need. As long as we stay intimate and dependent on God, we won't lose His good things—His promises of salvation, healing, wisdom, blessings, increase and much more.

The Bible says we don't have because we don't ask (James 4:2). Start asking God

✱ for what you need. If you need wisdom to parent your child, ask God. If you need salvation for family members, ask God. If you need your finances to turn around, be obedient to His Word and ask God.

Many of us don't really believe God's promises, or at least we don't believe they are intended for us. We think, *God gave that person what she needed, but He won't help me.* These thoughts usually come from our experiences with people who let us down, from the enemy who loves to put doubt in our minds about God's faithfulness or from our ignorance of His Word.

Don't allow yourself to become depressed over losing things.

The Bible tells us that the things of this world will pass away, so we shouldn't hold on to them too tightly. Don't allow yourself to become depressed over losing things. Grieve whatever loss is involved, and then trust God to meet your needs and to fulfill His promises. Through Him you'll find what you need.

Overcoming Depression

How do we overcome depression? Let's recap what we have learned so far:

1. Acknowledge the depression (Prov. 12:25).

2. Trust in God to help you (Ps. 46:1).

3. Praise Him despite the circumstances (Ps. 34:1).

4. Speak hope into the situation (Ps. 39:7).

5. Renew your negative thoughts through the positive Word of God (Phil. 4:8). Meditate on the goodness of God.

6. Take steps to correct your behavior. Take care of your body and get active. Make yourself *do* it. Don't wait to *feel* it.

7. Address the causes of the depression. For example, deal with anger, settle family conflicts, resolve inappropriate guilt and

forgive those who hurt you. If a lie is at the root of your thinking, <u>ask Jesus to speak His truth.</u>

~~~~~~~~~

Let the redeemed of the LORD say so!

—PSALM 107:2, NKJV

If you are a child of God, the Lord has redeemed you. What does it mean to be redeemed? It means you were bought with a price. You have been taken out of slavery and bondage by a Kinsman/Redeemer—Christ. While you were a slave to sin, He bought you with His blood sacrifice on the cross. Because of His blood, you are now redeemed—no longer a slave but a joint heir with Christ.

You've inherited all the good things of God, including a sound mind.

Christ came to redeem you from the curse of the Law.

44

Redeemed From the Curse of the Law

Read Deuteronomy 28 (NLT) to understand from what you have been redeemed. Many things related to depression are mentioned:

- External need (v. 17)
- Barrenness (v. 18)
- Confusion, disillusionment (v. 20)
- Disease (vv. 21–22, 27)
- Defeat (v. 25)
- Madness and panic (v. 28)
- Failure, bankruptcy and loss (vv. 29–31)
- Broken relationships (v. 30)
- Oppression and harsh treatment (v. 33)
- Hostility toward siblings and spouses (vv. 54–55)
- Anguish of the soul (v. 65)
- Lack of security and rest (v. 65)
- Doubt and no assurance of life (v. 66)
- Fear that terrifies your heart (vv. 66–67)

Christ took all these curses to the cross so that you could be free of them. As the redeemed of the Lord, you must say it is so! The next time you start to feel depressed, say, "I am redeemed by the blood of Jesus. I am not under the curse. He came to redeem me. Therefore, depression must leave me. I am the head, not the tail. I am above, not below. No weapon formed against me will prosper."

Claim your inheritance as a child of God. You've inherited all the good things of God, including a sound mind. Follow the advice of Psalm 107, and say that you are redeemed. _Then act redeemed._ Think on the good things of God. Speak His promises daily, and determine to have all He has for you. As you truly see yourself as the redeemed of the Lord, you will move out of that dark place of depression and into His glorious light.

Because we live after the Fall, difficulty will come. We can't live our lives without experiencing heartache, loss and disappointment, but the words of Paul remind us of this one fact: "We are hard pressed on every side, but not crushed; perplexed, but not in despair" (2 Cor. 4:8).

BREAKING FREE
PRAYER FOR YOU

Lord, You are the truth and the way. Whatever blocks me from believing this needs to be removed. Speak truth where there are lies. I will praise You for who You are, not for what I want You to do. Help me to value the things that are eternal and to live my life as one who has been redeemed. Most importantly, I want to become intimate with You. As I know and experience You, my life will be transformed.

CHAPTER 4

THE BODY AND DEPRESSION

Troubles are often the tools by which God fashions us for better things.

—HENRY WARD BEECHER

Since depression can be caused by physical and medical conditions, I recommend that you have a complete physical examination by a qualified physician before you begin any course of action. Remember that mood is affected by biochemical factors, and depression can be a side effect of disease and medications.

In this chapter I will briefly review some of the physical treatments for depression. Please understand that I am not recommending these treatments to you. But I do want to provide basic information so you can pray and seek counsel about what to do.

ANTIDEPRESSANTS

You have probably heard of serotonin, epinephrine, norepinephrine and other neurochemicals related to mood. Scientists are trying to determine just how these neurotransmitters interact with mood. What we do know is that drugs called *antidepressants* often improve mood because they work on these brain chemicals.

Since there is so much controversy in the church about the use of antidepressants, this topic is worthy of discussion. Talk to your physician, counselor and those who know you. God will help you decide if this is a course of action to consider.

Antidepressants are the most commonly prescribed treatment for depression. You should be aware, however, that there is evidence that talk therapy can be as effective as using medication for some types of depression.[1] "Talk therapy" is when you talk with a counselor or therapist with the purpose of relieving depression. Usually

> God will help you decide if the use of antidepressants is a course of action to consider.

goals are set, thoughts are examined, and behavior change is targeted. Talk therapy helps you understand the roots of your depression and make necessary changes. Talk therapies that focus on interpersonal issues and thoughts and behaviors related to depression are most beneficial. Change may not happen immediately, but tends to be long lasting with this approach.

In the chart on page 52, I've listed a few examples of the brand-name drugs used to treat depression. These lists are not exhaustive, and I am not recommending any of these drugs specifically. People often ask why there are so many antidepressants available and how a physician chooses which one to prescribe.

One reason antidepressants are so controversial is that people don't understand what they do.

There are many factors your physician takes into account when prescribing an antidepressant—your unique body chemistry, family history, current medications and much more. Different antidepressants work for different people. Sometimes it takes trial and error to determine the best one with the fewest side effects. The dosage may have to be adjusted to find an optimum level as well. And an antidepressant can take weeks before the full therapeutic effect is felt. Antidepressants should always be prescribed by a physician. They should never be borrowed or mixed without consulting your doctor.

One reason antidepressants are so controversial is that people don't understand what they do. They are not addictive like other classes of drugs. The purpose for taking an antidepressant is to correct your brain chemistry, which then stabilizes your mood. These medications basically help the brain do what it is supposed to do. When someone is depressed, neurotransmitters in the brain can become depleted, and these medications restore these neurotransmitters to the proper levels. Different classes of antidepressants work on different neurotransmitters in the brain. All of them work to restore brain function to better levels.

Categories of Antidepressants

Antidepressants usually fit into these four categories:

1. *Tricyclics* (e.g., Elavil, Tofranil, Norpramin, Sinequan and Pamelor). These drugs have been around awhile (since the 1960s) and typically have more unpleasant side effects than the newer ones.

2. *Monoamine oxidase inhibitors (MAO inhibitors)* (e.g., Marplan, Nardil and Parnate). This class of medications is used less often because of the potentially serious side effects, but it may be the one type of antidepressant that works for you. Your physician will discuss a special diet because of the potential rise in blood pressure with certain foods like wine, beer and cheeses and the interactions with other medications such as decongestants.

3. *Selective serotonin reuptake inhibitors (SSRIs)* (e.g., Paxil, Prozac, Zoloft, Luvox, Effexor and Celexa). These newer drugs usually have fewer and less severe side effects. The most common side effects are nausea, insomnia, agitation, headaches and sexual dysfunction.

4. *Other antidepressants in their own classes* such as Wellbutrin SR, Desyrel, Remeron and Ludiomil.

BIPOLAR DISORDER MEDICATIONS

For treating bipolar disorder, mood-stabilizing medications such as lithium are used. Lithium smooths out mood swings. It must be prescribed carefully because of potential toxicity. Other mood-stabilizing anticonvulsants such as Tegretol and Depakote are also used for bipolar disorder. On occasion doctors prescribe atypical antipsychotics like Zyprexa and Risperdal.

The challenge for people with bipolar disorder is to remain stable or to recover quickly from a manic-depressive episode. Standard treatment includes a medication regime because manic-depression is generally considered to be biologically based.

When it comes to treating bipolar disorder, a series of new studies speaks to the importance of addressing psychosocial factors. One of those factors is social support. A study in the November 1999 *Journal of Abnormal Psychology* reported family and friend support to be a key in shortening recovery from an episode.

Also, if you are bipolar and go through a period of stress, and are a negative thinker, you can set yourself up for a manic or depressive episode. So keep stress to a minimum, and renew your mind using biblical prescriptions (chapter three).

Finally, it is important to have consistent treatment when dealing with bipolar disorder. A regular sleep schedule and routine help tremendously. And it helps if you can learn to self-monitor your behavior.

In summary, lack of social support, negative thinking and stress, inconsistent treatment and changes in sleep patterns can set you up for failure if you have bipolar disorder. Pay attention to these areas of your life. Work on establishing a routine, and change your thinking. Even if the disorder is biologically based, there is still much

If you are bipolar, keep stress to a minimum, and renew your mind using biblical prescriptions.

you can do to stabilize your life. And again, healing is possible through Christ.

BREAKING FREE

MENTAL HEALTH FACT

Does Taking an Antidepressant Mean You Lack Faith in God?

If you are clinically depressed, you may find yourself struggling with this question. In today's world, the quick and easy solution for pain is to pop a pill. Medications can be abused and used to cover emotional pain, not resolve it. At other times, medications can assist the healing process. The question so often asked is, "Can God and medications coexist?"

To answer, one must first understand that depression has many causes (including biochemical). It can be brought on by stress, learned helplessness, relationship problems, feelings of powerlessness, work problems, failed expectations and loss, to name only a few. If you treat depression by medicating yourself and not working on the underlying or surrounding issues, you are only managing symptoms.

Symptom management is appropriate when you are severely clinically depressed, suicidal and not responding to therapy. Your choice isn't medication or God. One doesn't have to exclude the other. Antidepressants don't replace spirituality, but they can improve mood enough for you to revitalize your spiritual and emotional life.

Antidepressants are simply agents used to get you functioning again and to restore proper chemical balance in the brain. They are not magical cures that allow you to ignore the root causes of clinical depression.

God is our healer even though human

hands and medicine frequently play a role. Biblically, we are instructed to pray and ask for healing. Trusting God, however, doesn't preclude taking medical action. Is injecting insulin a lack of faith for the healing of diabetes? Or is taking an antihistamine during allergy season a lack of faith in God? No.

I believe God heals. The road to healing includes both miracles and the use of modern medicine. The key is to trust God and use what's available.

Build your faith through the Word of God. Put on that garment of praise for the spirit of despair (Isa. 61:3). This means we must take spiritual action. A garment is a covering we put on daily. So daily speak the goodness of God

The road to healing includes both miracles and the use of modern medicine.

over the depression. Claim His promise for a sound mind and peace. Stand on the Word no matter how you feel.

If you find you need medication along the way, you haven't let God down. Use what you need. Determine, though, to depend on God and to stand in faith. God sees your heart. <u>Be willing to explore all aspects of the depression and to resolve them. For example, are you holding on to anger and unforgiveness? Are you not getting enough sleep and running yourself down? Do you think negatively about most situations? Do you need to change your behavior?</u>

If an antidepressant helps you through a dark time or pulls you out of that black hole of despair, don't live in condemnation for using it. <u>Continue to renew your mind, behave according to God's Word and trust God for complete healing.</u>

ELECTRO-CONVULSIVE (SHOCK) TREATMENT (ECT)

Just the name of this treatment brings terrifying images into the minds of most people. We picture people strapped to a table, shaking violently and foaming at the mouth, then dragged out of the room to remain zombie-like for days. Fortunately, today's version of this treatment is nothing like our imaginations.

ECT is considered safe and effective for *severe* depression. The process works like this: "You receive a light general anesthesia and a muscle relaxant. An electric current is passed through your brain for 1 to 3 seconds. The stimulus causes a controlled seizure, which typically lasts for 20 to 90 seconds. You wake up in 5 to 10 minutes and rest for about half an hour. Most people require 6 to 10 treatments."[2]

Researchers aren't sure why this treatment works as it does, but it appears to be effective for those at high risk for suicide. And for those severely depressed elderly adults who can't take medications because of heart disease, this treatment is available.

CHANGING SLEEP SCHEDULES

Not only does depression cause sleep problems, but also insomnia can cause depression. It is important to get enough regular sleep. If you are experiencing sleep problems, there are simple things you can do that may help. Limit alcohol and caffeine intake, and get more exercise. Try reading before bed. Don't take naps during the day, and try to establish a good sleep routine and schedule.

DIETARY CHANGES

✗ Eating a healthy diet is important in com-
bating depression. Symptoms of depression
can be caused by deficiencies in folic acid
and vitamin B_{12}. Low levels of both may
also lead to a poorer response to antidepressant medications.[3] So many of us have
poor eating habits and don't get the nutrition our body needs to function properly.

There are studies investigating the use of
omega-3 fatty acids (found in fish oil and
certain plants) as mood stabilizers and as
possible relapse prevention for people with
bipolar disorder.[4] So you may try eating
more fish to see if you notice a difference.

EXERCISE

A meta review of fourteen controlled studies published in *Professional Psychology:
Research and Practice* in June of 1999
✗ found that regular exercise worked as well
as cognitive therapy in treating mild to
moderate depression.[5] Something as simple as exercise helps to alleviate symptoms
of depression. The benefits of exercise
continue to be important for total health,

and yet so few of us take advantage of this benefit.

LIGHT EXPOSURE

Light therapy is especially effective in the treatment of SAD. Light interacts with the eye through the optic nerve and increases brain chemicals that alleviate depression. This doesn't mean you can sit anywhere there is light and feel better. Regular indoor lighting isn't intense enough to be effective (only 300–500 lux). You need something intense like a fluorescent light bulb. Some people feel full-spectrum light is best because it is similar to sunlight. It provides about 2500 lux, which is what you need.[6]

You can use a commercial lighting device or a fluorescent light box. Some insurance companies will even reimburse you for a light box. Or try thirty minutes of morning light by walking outside or sitting under a fluorescent or full-spectrum light while working or watching TV. Don't stare into the light, though. You'll just get a headache doing that!

A German study found that light might

even help those without SAD, although this is still being studied.[7] Other psychiatric disorders such as eating disorders and obsessive-compulsive disorders might potentially benefit from light.

Don't confuse the symptoms of SAD with other conditions like diabetes or high blood pressure. See a doctor to be sure SAD is the cause of your problems. <u>If you suffer from severe depression, consult a mental health professional.</u> Light won't hurt you, but it may not help you either.

If you are someone who suffers from SAD, light therapy should be the first step in treatment. And hey, a trip to the Bahamas come mid-January couldn't hurt any of us!

HERBS AND ALTERNATIVE MEDICINE

Herbal treatments are very popular but should *never* be taken with any medication or supplement without providing a full medical history, including current medications, to your doctor and pharmacist.

One very popular herb that is often used to treat mild and moderate depression is St. John's wort. This herb comes from a low, shrubby plant with yellow flowers and has been studied in Europe. There are side effects associated with St. John's wort. The most common are dry mouth, dizziness, gastrointestinal symptoms, fatigue and increased sensitivity to sunlight. This herb can also negatively interact with other medications.

German studies tout the herb as effective as other antidepressant medications. And the Council for Responsible Nutrition reports it is safe for mild and moderate depression. However, studies are currently under way at the National Institutes of Health comparing St. John's wort with placebo (nothing), talk therapy and an antidepressant drug (Zoloft). One initial result was that St. John's wort was ineffective for treating major depression with moderate symptoms.[8] So again, certain types of depression may respond to different treatments. Studies on the effectiveness of St. John's wort continue in order to determine the best use of this herb for depression.

Discuss herbal and alternative therapies

with your doctor. Natural remedies are not regulated by the Food and Drug Administration, and so they vary from bottle to bottle. Natural remedies can still cause side effects and be interactive with other medications you take, so make sure you are under the care of someone who can follow your progress.

There is much interest in alternative forms of medicine. It is not the purpose of this book to review all the options currently used. I am not a physician or alternative medicine expert. I simply want to inform you that there are a number of alternative treatments, some of them popular but without proven effectiveness.

> *My advice is to seek wise counsel and ask the Holy Spirit to lead you.*

SAM-e

SAM-e (pronounced Sammy) is usually sold over the counter as a dietary supplement. It is a chemical substance found in all human cells. The belief is that SAM-e increases levels of serotonin and dopamine (two neurotransmitters), but this is yet to be proven. And one has to be careful not to take too much as it is possible to elevate serotonin to too high of a level. Side effects are usually mild and can include mania. As a result, someone with bipolar disorder should exercise caution as mania is already part of that disorder. Studies are underway to prove or disprove the claims made by taking this substance. Many feel it is effective for mild and moderate depression.

5-HTP

There is a chemical in your body needed to make serotonin, a neurotransmitter involved in mood. That chemical is called 5-HTP. It is another over-the-counter supplement used to treat depression and is considered a serotonin booster. Again, more studies proving the claims of this chemical need to be conducted.

Omega-3 fatty acids

You may have seen fish oil capsules containing omega-3 fatty acids sold in stores. These capsules are usually high in fat and can cause gastrointestinal problems. Omega-3 fatty acids are found naturally in fish like salmon and halibut and in flaxseed oil. The theory is that some people with depression have decreased amounts of an active ingredient found in omega-3 fatty acids. By eating more fish or taking the capsules, this ingredient is boosted and may stabilize mood. This may be especially true for people with bipolar depression. Again, more studies are needed to bear out various claims. Since American diets tend to be low in omega-3 fatty acids, it certainly can't hurt any of us to eat more fish and sprinkle a little ground flaxseed on our cereal.

What I've presented are the most common options that address your physical body. From treating people in therapy, I know how difficult making decisions in this area can be. My advice is to seek wise counsel and ask the Holy Spirit to lead you. If you want to investigate these options, <u>find someone who can treat you competently and safely and who stays abreast of research.</u>

Lord, I want to be led by You as I pursue healing. Help me do those things that work toward building better physical and mental health. Help me examine those areas of my life in need of change. Lead me by Your Holy Spirit when it comes to making decisions about treatments. I trust You will give me peace about the direction to take.

CHAPTER 5

THE MIND AND EMOTIONS

The best cure for worry, depression, melancholy and brooding is to go deliberately forth and try to lift with one's sympathy the gloom of somebody else.

—ARNOLD BENNETT

Depression is fought mostly in the mind. Our thinking affects how we feel and how we perceive the world. When you are depressed, your thinking is negative and lacks hope. It needs to be renewed. The work to be done is removing the lies of the enemy in order to live in God's truth.

In my experience, it is not enough for people to be told how to change their thinking. People need an encounter with the living God in order to change. When God fills you with His truth, and you experience His love firsthand, it is transforming.

God desires to move you out of depression and into the joy of living. With Him by your side, you can face loss and learn to cope with unpleasant feelings, especially those of sadness and hopelessness. Areas of past hurt can be healed.

BREAK FREE FROM GRIEF

Depression can be brought on by unresolved grief. At times we experience loss and try to cover up the pain. We may feel we have to be strong, or we may believe we can't face pain without falling apart. Sometimes we think that crying and sadness are signs of weakness and not appropriate to express. At other times we may try to numb emotional pain through alcohol, drugs or other distractions and addictions.

> *God desires to move you out of depression and into the joy of living.*

Dealing With Loss

If you have experienced loss, make sure you allow grief to be expressed and that you have followed these steps:

1. *Acknowledge the loss you experienced.* Does your depression stem from a loss of relationship, situation or dream? If so, specify the loss. It may be a divorce, a death, loss of health, the dream of marriage or children, or some other situation. Don't try to minimize it or to pretend it is no big deal. Loss is painful.

2. *Identify how you feel about the loss.* Are you sad, empty, lonely, hurt or disappointed? Don't stuff those feelings inside. Hidden feelings become problematic for the mind and body. Whatever your feelings, they are neither *right* nor *wrong.* They are just how you feel. Express it to God and/or a trusted person. Reading the Book of Psalms may

help to put you in touch with feelings of loss.

3. *Grieve and release your loss to God.* It is important to grieve the loss you feel and to release it to God. You may feel shock, denial, confusion, sadness, numbness, irritability, hopelessness, helplessness, fear, isolation, loneliness, emptiness, disorganization or guilt. These feelings come and go. Allow them to surface and to be expressed. God knows your pain and will walk you through it. As you move through the grieving process, ask God to heal the pain.

~~~~~~~~~~

BREAK FREE FROM NEGATIVE THINKING

Depression isn't always a result of getting stuck in grieving a loss. It can be rooted in other causes, as we saw in chapter one. The most common cause of depression is negative thinking, which leads to negative emotions, which create negative perceptions, which influence negative thinking.

71 A vicious cycle!

Do you remember the cycle that goes round and round from chapter one?

<u>In order to break free from depression, your thinking must change.</u> The thoughts of a depressed person are negative, hopeless, helpless and filled with doom and gloom. <u>These thoughts are born out of lies the enemy has implanted in us, usually at times of emotional wounding or hurt.</u>

So use these steps to break free:

1. *Identify depression triggers.* What sets off that <u>bad feeling?</u> Is it something someone said, a thought you had, a problem, a situation or the actions of another person? Use the chart on page 77 to track depressive feelings. Under *Trigger,* jot down the cue that sets off feelings of depression.

2. *Identify the emotion felt.* Most likely it will be depression, <u>intense sadness,</u> <u>hurt</u> or <u>anger.</u> Write down the emotion.

3. *Write down the thought you have when you feel this emotion.* <u>Your thinking is the source of the problem.</u> You may be thinking, *I'll*

*never get through this. No one
likes me or wants to be with me.
I'm not worth anything. I'm not
even loveable!* Identify your automatic thought. It will be negative
and based on a lie.

4. *Pray and ask Christ to bring truth
to you.* In Christ, nothing is hopeless. He is there to guide and
strengthen you. He sees you as
one of His creation whom He has
chosen. But you must experience
that revelation firsthand. So ask
Him to speak truth to you, and
He will. Once He does, your
thoughts will be renewed.

5. *Write down the renewed thought.*
The truth of Jesus Christ brings
renewal to our minds. Write
down what you hear in prayer
through an impression, a voice, a
revelation, a word picture, the
Word of God. Whatever the truth
is, write it down.

6. *Revisit the emotion.* After your
thought has changed and God has
spoken truth into your situation,
revisit that situation. Hopefully
the depression has lifted. If not,

there may be more thoughts with which to work.

7. *Begin to walk in healing with new actions and behavior.* When your thinking changes, your behavior will follow. Instead of doing things associated with depression, you will choose actions consistent with improved mood. You may talk to a friend, go to an event, be more assertive, start to make plans or take some other positive action. The opposite of depression is usually action. Take action.

BREAKING   F R E E

MENTAL HEALTH FACT

Depression Tracking Chart

Here is an example: Sally feels depressed every Friday night. She overeats and sits in front of the television. Then she goes to bed but can't sleep.

Trigger: Sally is twenty-two and feels she should be out on a date on Friday nights. For the past two months, no one has asked her out. The trigger is Friday night date night.

Emotion: Lonely and hurt

Automatic thought: *I'll never get married. I'll spend the rest of my life alone. I must be a loser.*

Behavior: Sally isolates herself in front of the TV while overeating.

Renewed thought after prayer: *Christ loves me, and He reminded me that my future is in His hands. My steps are ordered by Him. Not having a Friday night date doesn't mean that I am a loser.*

Revisit the emotion. I no longer feel depressed.

New action: Stop sitting at home and sulking. Overeating isn't helping me feel better; it just gives me an immediate way to feel good. Instead, I'll go to a coffeehouse Friday night with a girlfriend. And who knows...maybe I'll meet someone there as well. If not, I'll have a nice time with a friend.

Use the chart on page 77 to begin tracking your depressive thoughts and to make changes. It can be used as a journal or record of thoughts that need renewal. So

Jesus Christ is the One who transforms and heals us.

often, we try to change our thoughts on our own and struggle to see things differently. Invite Christ into the self dialogue. Ask Him to reveal His truth to you. He is the One who transforms and heals us.

AREAS FOR CHANGE

Once you change your thinking, there may be other areas of your life in need of change. Check each of these areas as well.

1. Forgive those who have hurt you or let you down.

Forgiveness is an individual act. Choose to forgive even when people don't deserve it or have not asked for your forgiveness. Unforgiveness can be a root of depression and can lead to bitterness and hardness of heart. Forgiveness is not the same as reconciliation. Reconciliation takes two people. But you can make a decision to forgive even when the other person doesn't cooperate.

Forgiveness is something you give to another person because Christ gave it to you. You didn't earn His forgiveness, but He gave it anyway. Forgiveness not only releases the other person from an offense,

76

DEPRESSION TRACKING CHART				
Trigger What cued the emotion?	Emotion	Automatic Thought		Behavior What did you do?
Renewed Thought Truth	Revisit the Emotion What do you feel now?			New Behavior What will (or did) you do?

but it also releases you from hanging on to the offense. And even though you choose to forgive, the feelings associated with the hurt or offense can stay with you for awhile. Hurtful words, actions and emotions usually take time to heal. It also takes time to build trust after a hurtful experience. The goal, however, is eventually to release negative emotion (e.g., anger, resentment) and thoughts (e.g., judgment) toward the person who hurt you.

> *Forgiveness is something you give to another person because Christ gave it to you.*

2. Deal with sin in your life.

Any area of your life that doesn't line up with God's directives should be confessed and changed. Depression can be a result of unconfessed sin and ongoing disobedience to God's Word or direction. Many of the people I've counseled are running from God in a Jonah-like experience. They wonder why they feel so depressed, and yet they are avoiding the call on their lives or living in willful disobedience.

3. Avoid blaming others.

People can certainly influence you and your behavior, but you are responsible for how you live your life. Don't blame others for your pain. Others may be the source of your pain, as in the case of abuse, but your response is what ultimately matters to God. Will you blame others for feeling depressed, or will you acknowledge what others have done, forgive them and live in joy?

Perhaps you are hiding behind blame and won't take action to get better. Maybe you prefer to focus on the injustice of the world and others and not look at your reaction. We all experience loss and pain. Like Job, the test is whether or not we will be faithful. Will we allow the pain to draw us *toward* God or *away* from Him?

4. Change your expectations.

Don't expect life to happen without loss or disappointment. If you do, it's a setup for depression. You can't control circumstances, and you can't control other people's behavior. But you can develop more realistic expectations. People will let you down and not behave nicely all the time. Bad things happen in this fallen world in which we live. But you can expect God to be with you through any bad time. He promises to walk through the valleys.

5. Stop hanging out with negative people.

When you are depressed, negative people don't help improve your mood. In fact, when you spend time with people who complain and see life through a negative lens, you feel even worse. So try to spend more time around people who will encourage you and who don't easily give in to defeat. It is possible to have a positive outlook on life because we know that God holds our future.

Depressed people who have "learned helplessness" must learn when to say no and to set appropriate boundaries.

6. Don't allow yourself to feel stigmatized over using medication.

If medication is helping you, don't listen to the uninformed opinions of others. Seek wise counsel, pray and ask God to direct your healing. If medication is a part of that process, it's OK to use it.

7. *Become more assertive.*

A common problem associated with depression is being too passive. When you don't speak up, thus allowing others to walk all over you, you feel helpless. You may also secretly harbor anger and resentment as well.

Depressed people who have "learned helplessness" must learn when to say *no* and to set appropriate boundaries. People cannot read your mind or know what you need unless you tell them. So assertiveness skills are important to develop in order to meet your needs, set limits and take charge of your life where and when you can.

Next time you feel depressed because you failed to be assertive, practice this skill. It will get easier the more you do it. The end result will be a happier you!

8. *Problem solve.*

One of the problems with depression is that you don't see a solution to a presenting problem. Instead, the situation or future looks dim and hopeless. Hopelessness is not of God. We always have hope because we serve the God of the possible. Therefore, even in the darkest moment or time, you need to hold on to hope in Christ. His promise is to provide a way when there is no way.

It also helps to approach difficulty with a problem-solving attitude. One way to combat depression is to become a good problem-solver.

BREAKING FREE

MENTAL HEALTH FACT

Become a Good Problem-Solver

When a problem comes your way:

- *Define the problem.* Get a clear definition in your head as to what the actual difficulty may be. For example, the problem isn't that you married a lazy man. The problem is that he doesn't take out the trash at night. Be specific, and focus on the behavior. Then clearly define the behavior so you aren't working with some nebulous thing. If you define the problem, you'll know what you need to change.

- *How often or how long is it happening?* Measure the number of times the problem occurs or the length of time it goes on. This way you will have an accurate count or duration of the problem. This is important because you need to measure change. Too many of us don't recognize small changes in the right direction.

- *Do something.* Time to intervene. Instead of responding the way you always do or in a way that doesn't promote change, try a new strategy. For example, instead of going to your room and talking to no one, force yourself to call a friend and ask how she is doing. Stop doing the thing that doesn't work, and try a new tactic. You can experiment until you find something that works.

- *Evaluate how well things are going.* If you have a clear definition of the problem, measure how much of a problem it is and then do something, you can see if the behavior gets better or worse or happens less or more. If your husband is taking out the trash two out of three weeks, and he never did it before, you've made progress. Change is usually a step-by-step process that needs lots of encouragement.

- *If what you are doing doesn't work, try another tactic.* The secret here is not to panic or give up. You tried something, and it didn't work. Try something else. Talk to other people, a counselor or family members, and get input if you need it. Just because you don't see a solution doesn't mean there isn't one. There is always a way. Remember that God has also promised to make a way where there is no way, so don't panic or give up.

~~~~~~~~~~

Practice problem solving. It will boost your confidence and reduce stress. Next time you encounter hopelessness say, "I can deal with this. It's just a matter of finding the right solution."

✱ 9. Manage your emotions—don't let them manage you.

You will feel loss and pain as a response to things that happen in life. The goal is to manage negative emotions without them depressing you. You can have a negative feeling like anger or sadness, but you don't want to get stuck in those feelings. Remember that when we get stuck in depression, it is usually because a lie has ✱ been implanted at the time of hurt or wounding.

> *Practice problem solving. It will boost your confidence and reduce stress.*

10. Do something for someone else.

Doing for others usually improves mood. It gets your mind off your own problems and is action in a positive direction.

11. Get support.

The worse thing you can do when you are feeling depressed is to isolate yourself. Support is a buffer for depression. Talk with people. Let family and friends help. It also helps to have people who will pray with you, encourage you and remind you of God's promises. Be connected.

✶ 12. Accept God's love for you.

If you have trouble believing that God loves you or cares about you, ask Him to make that real. It is vital for you to experience God's unconditional love.

✶ 13. Trust in God.

People will let you down, but God never will. It is easier to trust someone you know well, so spend time with your Father. Get to know Him. He will never disappoint. He cares intimately about your life. There is joy in knowing Him. He is faithful and worthy of your trust.

✶ 14. Break overwhelming tasks into small steps.

When you feel overwhelmed by a task, break it down into small, manageable steps. Set priorities, and do what you can. There is evidence that links certain types of perfectionism with depression.[1] So don't try to be perfect.

15. Stay connected.

When people are depressed, they isolate. This only makes the depression worse and creates fertile ground for the enemy to start working on your mind. Stay connected to people. Force yourself to socialize and be around others even if you don't feel like it.

16. Work on interpersonal relationships.

Depression is often rooted in relationship problems. Work on restoring relationships and improving troubled ones. Forgive those who have hurt you. If you need a marital or family therapist to help you make changes and confront conflicts, don't be afraid to go to therapy. Jesus tells us to be reconciled to each other.

Lord, renew my mind. Speak Your truth to me. I want to be free today. As I heal from these negative thoughts that have caused depressive feelings, I can see my life differently because of Your light. Please bring Your light into my darkness, renewing my mind and healing the emotional pain. I trust You and want to experience joy and gladness as promised in Your Word.

CHAPTER 6

BREAKING FREE SUMMARY

Therefore the redeemed of the LORD shall return, and come with singing unto Zion; and everlasting joy shall be upon their head; they shall obtain gladness and joy; and sorrow and mourning shall flee away.

—ISAIAH 51:11, KJV

When you face depression, here is a brief review of what we have covered:

1. Acknowledge the depression (Prov. 12:25).

2. Trust God to help you (Ps. 46:1).

3. Praise Him despite the circumstances (Ps. 34:1).

4. Speak hope into the situation (Ps. 39:7). He is your hope.

Invite Him into your self-talk through prayer.

5. Renew your negative thoughts by asking God to speak truth to you. Think on good things (Phil. 4:8). Stand on His Word.

6. Take steps to correct your behavior. Take care of your body, and get active. Make yourself *take action*. Don't wait to *feel* it.

7. Address the causes of the depression. For example, deal with anger, settle family conflicts, resolve inappropriate guilt and forgive those who hurt you.

8. Spend time with your Father. Get to know Him intimately. In His presence, there is fullness of joy.

9. Praise Him because He's already done everything you need.

10. Be transformed by the ongoing renewing of your mind.

As you face your everyday life, recognize loss. (Things and people are not always what or who we wish them to be.) Feel the emotions that accompany loss (sadness, anger, hurt, disappointment and others). Renew your thoughts (replace lies with God's truth), and release your emotional pain to God. Unless you do these things, you may find yourself depressed.

Fortunately we serve a God who knows our emotional lives intimately. He can take any loss and work it for our good. That's His way. He sent His Son, Jesus, to die (major loss) for us. Jesus transformed death to new life. Allow God to transform you by His glorious light. In the light, there is no darkness—therefore, no depression.

THE HOPE

The LORD is my strength and my shield; my heart trusts in him, and I am helped. My heart leaps for joy and I will give thanks to him in song.

—PSALM 28:7

I love the Book of Psalms. There is such emotional passion in those verses. The writers experienced hope and despair, joy and rage, confidence and fear, certainty and doubt. Feelings flowed out of their life experiences and remind us how easily our emotions ebb and flow. As we read the often pain-filled words, we don't feel so alone.

In Psalm 22, David felt abandoned and helpless, ignored, despised and rejected, ridiculed for his faith, taunted by vicious enemies, distressed, on the verge of death and entrapped. Still, David believed that

God was near and would deliver him. His hope was in God, not in his abilities, other people or even his own strength. As a result, he didn't remain in despair.

This psalm is a powerful prophetic glimpse into the agony Jesus would experience. And in his life, David too tasted deep suffering, yet he chose to put his trust and faith in God. Perhaps you feel as David did and can relate to his wide range of emotional distresses. If so, do what David did—believe that God will rescue you. Praise Him and shout for joy. Dance before your Maker.

God does not want you depressed. He wants you free and experiencing His joy. The word *joy* is found 150 times in the Bible and comes from our intimate walk with God. It is not something we conjure up with self-help books or our will. It is not something I can instruct you how to feel. And it is not dependent on other people or circumstances. Joy comes from the Lord, and it is our strength.

A fruit of the Spirit is joy. The Bible tells us to shout for joy, sing praises to the Lord, put on the garment of praise for the spirit of heaviness and put on this strength (joy). Trials will come, but we are to count them all joy, knowing that our faith is being tested, and it will produce patience. (See James 1.) Yes, there will be weeping and sadness, but joy comes in the morning.

Let the joy of the Lord be your strength. If you want this joy, ask God to take you to your place of pain, speak His truth, love you with His everlasting love, and He will set you free. Walk intimately with Him, allowing Him to renew your mind. Not only will you break free from depression, but you will also break forth in joy!

God does not want you depressed. He wants you free and experiencing His joy.

> We will shout for joy when you are victorious and will lift up our banners in the name of our God. May the LORD grant all your requests.
>
> —PSALM 20:5

BREAKING  F R E E

PRAYER FOR YOU

Lord, thank You for taking me out of
darkness and into Your glorious light.

CHAPTER 1

1. "What is depression?" MayoClinic.com, retrieved June, 6, 2002, from www.mayoclinic.com/ivoke.cfm?id=DS00175.
2. "What is postpartum illness?" *Introduction to postpartum illness,* retrieved online July 5, 2002, from www.chss.iup.edu/postpartum/post-trial2.htm.
3. Ibid.
4. Ibid.
5. Depression descriptions adapted from the *Diagnostic and Statistical Manual of Mental Disorders,* 4th ed. (Washington DC: American Psychiatric Press, 1994).
6. R. Johnson and S. Somers, "NIMH, JAMA shed light on Seasonal Affective Disorder, *Psychiatric Times, MHi.,* February 1994, retrieved online June 22, 2002, from www.mhsource.com/pt/p940216.html.
7. Ibid.
8. "What is depression?" Retrieved June, 6, 2002, from www.mayoclinic.com/ivoke.cfm?id=DS00175.

CHAPTER 2

1. Diagnostic criteria from the *Diagnostic and Statistical Manual of Mental Disorders*.
2. Michael Yapko, Ph.D., "Clinical Update on Depression," *The American Association for Marriage and Family Therapy*, Volume 1, Issue 2, March 1999.
3. "Some things you should know about preventing teen suicide," American Academy of Pediatrics, retrieved online from www.aap.org/advocacy/child-healthmonth/prevteensuicide.htm.
4. F. Jones, "Statistical risk factors for suicide, *Monitor in Psychology*, Vol. 32, No. 10, November 2001, retrieved online from www.apa.org/monitor/nov01/suiciderisk.html.

CHAPTER 4

1. "Therapy may be as good as medication for depression," *MEDLINEplus*, retrieved online June 5, 2002, from www.nlm.nih.gov/medlineplus/news/fullstory_7761.html.
2. "What is depression?", MayoClinic.com, retrieved online June 6, 2002, from www.mayoclinic.com.
3. "Causes of depression, MayoClinic.com, November 15, 2002, retrieved online

June 30, 2002, from www.mayoclinic.com.

4. "Complementary and alternative medicine," MayoClinic.com, retrieved online June 6, 2002, from www.mayoclinic.com.

5. M. A. Tkachuk and G. L. Martin, "Exercise Therapy for Patients with Psychiatric Disorders, Research and Clinical Implications," *Professional Psychology: Research and Practice*, vol. 30, no. 3 (1999): 275–282.

6. Johnson and Somers, "NIMH, JAMA shed light on seasonal affective disorder," *Psychiatric Times,* retrieved online July 5, 2002 from www.mhsource.com/pt/p940216.html.

7. Ibid.

8. "National Institutes of Health." *NIH News,* April 9, 2002, release retrieved online June 5, 2002.

CHAPTER 5

1. APA online press release, "Researcher links perfectionism in high achievers with depression and suicide," *PsycNET 2002*, American Psychological Association, retrieved online June 4, 2002, from www.apa.org/releases/perfect.html.

Your Walk With God Can Be Even Deeper...

With *Charisma* magazine, you'll be informed and inspired by the features and stories about what the Holy Spirit is doing in the lives of believers today.

Each issue:
- Brings you exclusive world-wide reports to rejoice over.
- Keeps you informed on the latest news from a Christian perspective.
- Includes miracle-filled testimonies to build your faith.
- Gives you access to relevant teaching and exhortation from the most respected Christian leaders of our day.

Call 1-800-829-3346 for 3 FREE trial issues
Offer #A2CCHB

If you like what you see, then pay the invoice of $22.97 (**saving over 51% off the cover price**) and receive 9 more issues (12 in all). Otherwise, write "cancel" on the invoice, return it, and owe nothing.

Experience the Power of Spirit-Led Living

Charisma
& CHRISTIAN LIFE

Charisma Offer #A2CCHB
P.O. Box 420234
Palm Coast, Florida 32142-0234
www.charismamag.com